Hedge Fund
Trading Strategies
Detailed Explanation Of The
Hedged Short Condor
Index ETF
Derivative Income Spreads

AN INVESTING NEWSLETTER

HEDGE STRATEGIES

...offering impersonal, general and indirect opinion

™

A Moderate Strategy

ISBN 1451514727
EAN 978-1-451-51472-8

1. Hedge-Fund 2. Hedgefund 3. Condor 4. ETF
5. Exchange-Traded-Fund 6. Options 7. Investing
8. Strategies 9. Trading 10. Spreads 11. Derivatives 12. Short

Printed in the United States of America

STRATEGY DESCRIPTION AND EXPLANATION
For The
Hedged Short Condor Index ETF Derivative Income Spreads, a Moderate Strategy

It should not be assumed that this strategy will be profitable in the future or will equal the performance of the strategy examples as explained in this newsletter report.

- **When long the market, money is made if the market trades up.**
- **When short the market, money is made if the market trades down.**
- **When applying a Hedged Short Condor strategy, money is made if the market trades up, down or flat.**

The Hedged Short Condor Index ETF Derivative Income Spreads moderate strategy seeks to earn leveraged returns by applying short spreads at either end of an Index ETF price range. If the body of a condor with its wings outstretched is the current Index ETF market price and short spreads are its wings, this strategy looks like:

Objective
Through statistical probabilities this moderate strategy seeks to produce consistent monthly derivative income. In the visualization above, observe the green profit zone. As long as the Index ETF market price remains within the boundaries created by the sold put and sold call option contracts, full potential profit is achieved. Beyond these boundaries is partial profit to the hedge point, and then loss to the stop loss.

Statistical probabilities are used to determine the option strike prices for the boundary points at which each spread will yield full potential profit 95 out of 100 times.

The Rules, In Order Of Importance
(1) Profits are made only through a sale, never a purchase.
(2) Maintain short spread distances of 2 standard deviations.
(3) Trade only diversified instruments with low levels of volatility.
(4) Trade only diversified instruments with high levels of trading volume.
(5) Never deviate from the Guideposts.

What Is The Spread?
An investment is a security that is purchased. A position is a security that is sold. An investment position is a combination of both (purchased and sold).

A spread is an investment or position composed of two or more option contracts. At least one of the option contracts must be bought if the other contract(s) is sold. Option contracts can hedge other option contracts. When one option contract in a spread hedges the other option contract(s) it is referred to as the *hedging option*.

A spread is described by the difference between the identifying dollar amounts at which the two or more option contracts are written. The identifying dollar amounts are called strike prices.

For example: If the difference distance between spread strike prices is 100 cents, the spread is a $1 spread; 200 cents is a $2 spread; 250 cents is a $2.50 spread; and so on.

Call option contracts have higher incremental value the closer they are to zero. Put option contracts have higher incremental value the further they are from zero.

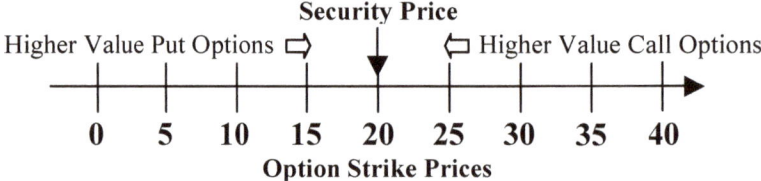

The option contracts at each strike price of a spread are added to each other to determine the '*cost*', or '*value*' or '*potential profit*' of a spread. The *cost* of a spread describes the calculation result when the spread is *long*, or

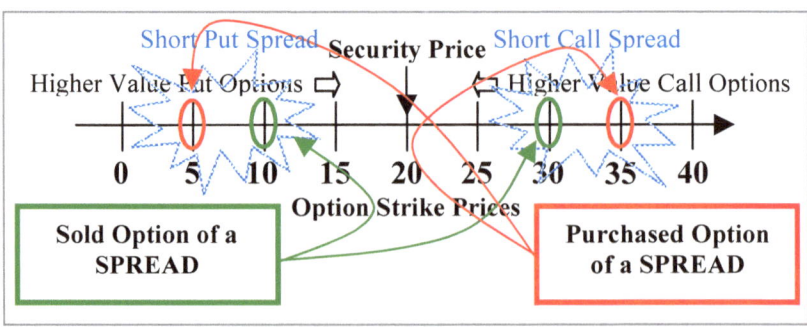

requires an input of monies, as in an investment. The *value* or *potential profit* of a spread describes the calculation result when the spread is *short,* or produces a surplus of monies, as in a position.

When the higher valued contract of the spread is sold and the lower valued contract of the spread is purchased as a hedge to the higher valued contract, this spread is said to be a '*short*', '*credit*', '*written*' or '*sold*' spread.

When the higher valued contract of the spread is purchased and the lower valued contract of the spread is sold as a hedge to the higher valued contract, this spread is said to be a '*long*' or '*debit*' spread.

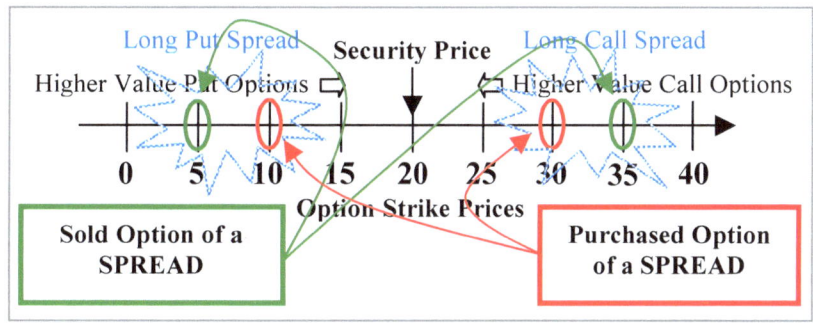

What Is An ETF?

ETF stands for exchange traded fund. These securities trade like stocks on an exchange. The ETF is composed of a basket of individual stocks. Index ETFs seek to mimic an index by holding the group of stocks that compose the index in a proportion appropriate to cause price values of an index ETF to move in tandem with the actual index values to an accuracy (correlation) of 98% or greater. Indices are the Dow Jones Industrial Average, Standard & Poor's 500 Index, Nasdaq 100, Wilshire 1000 and Russell 2000, to name a few.

Index ETF prices are a fraction of their mimicked index. The SPY is $1/10^{th}$ the value of the Standard and Poor's 500 Index. If the Standard and Poor's 500 Index is 1150, the SPY will be trading at approximately $115. By definition, indices are diversified, therefore Index ETFs are diversified. Index ETFs like the SPY, DIA and QQQQ representing the Standard and Poor's 500 Index, the Dow Jones Industrial Average and the NASDAQ 100 experience high levels of daily trading volume.

What Is A Hedge?

A hedge is an act, tool or means of preventing loss in one security with another partially or fully counter-balancing security. A hedge reduces the possibility of a loss of principal (value) due to adverse movements of the investment or position. If one security depreciates in value, the counter-balancing security will appreciate in value. Hedging provides degrees of protection. When hedge protection is purchased, the more expensive, the greater the hedge. A hedge may be realized through purchases of counter-balancing securities as well as through sales of counter-balancing securities. The profit from one side of a hedging pair of securities may be harvested and reset in a manner that still provides a hedge for the securities. Profits from the hedging pair of securities may be harvested whenever profitable to the strategy and supportive of the hedge.

For example: A hedge is considered to be *full, perfect, deep* or *counter-balancing* when there is no loss in value from price movements. A *shallow hedge* experiences loss in value (in red) from price movements.

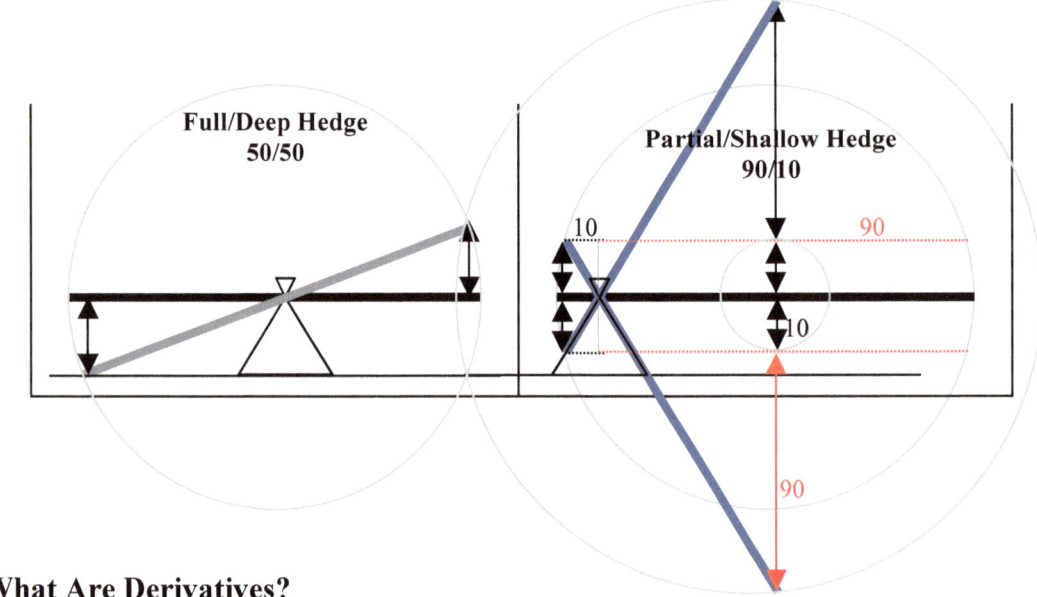

What Are Derivatives?
Derivatives are contracts or obligations that are bought or sold in trading markets. They derive their value from the movement of other securities, such as stocks, exchange traded funds (ETFs), bonds, commodities or currencies. Those securities are referred to as *underlying securities*.

An Index ETF is itself a derivative, because its value is based on the movements of the portfolio of stocks that form the index it mimics. By its definition, an index is diversified and possesses a low to moderate level of volatility.

Derivatives can be referred to as securities. Options are derivatives.

What Are Call And Put Options?
A *call option* is a contract issued by a seller to a buyer, giving the buyer the opportunity, but not the obligation, to buy 100 shares of a security at a contracted price (the *strike price*) and obligating the seller to sell to the buyer 100 shares of that security from which the call option derives its value.

A *put option* is a contract issued by a seller to a buyer, giving the buyer the right to sell 100 shares of a security at a contracted price (the *strike price*) and obligating the seller to purchase those 100 shares of the security from which the put option derives its value.

Anyone can be a seller of options. One does not have to have a special membership card or license. One only has to be able to fulfill the terms of the contract by owning 100 shares of the underlying security (obligated security) in the case of the sold call option, or by having enough cash to buy 100 shares of the underlying security (obligated security) in the case of the sold put option--also termed *hedging the short option*.

Call and put options can be either sold or purchased. It is often better to sell an option than to buy an option, because options have limited lives. They expire. Buying something that disappears into thin air is an unwise investment. Follow Rule (1): **Profits are made only through a sale, never a purchase**.

Option Components Are Composed Of:

(i)   **Strike Price** is the dollar amount at which the terms of the option contract obligation can be fulfilled. If a call option gives the buyer of the call option contract the opportunity, but not the obligation, to buy 100 shares of the underlying security at $50, then $50 is the strike price. Put and call option contracts are available at multiple strike prices along the underlying security value spectrum. Securities with lower values have option contract strike prices available every $1 or $2.50 in value from 0. The medium value securities have option contracts available at strike prices every $5 in value. High value securities have option contracts available at strike prices every $10 in value.

(ii)   **Premium** is the cost of an option. An option cost is composed of intrinsic value (true value) and time value (speculative value). This strategy sells option spreads that have only time value (speculative value).

(iii)   **Derivative Income** is profit for the seller of options equal to the time value of the option premium.

(iv)   **Option Valuation** is a function of the price movements of the option's underlying security plus its premium.

(v)   **Intrinsic Value** is the definable value of an option contract in relation to the strike price. If the strike price is $50 and the underlying security is trading at $54, the intrinsic value of the call option is $4. If the strike price is $50 and the underlying security is trading at $35, the intrinsic value of a put option is $15. A call option only has intrinsic value if the underlying security is trading above the call option strike price. A put option only has intrinsic value if the underlying security is trading below the put option strike price. Any value in the premium of an option that is not intrinsic value is time value (speculative value).

For example: If a put option contract was purchased at a strike price of $50 before the 100 shares of the already owned underlying security fell in value from $50 to $35, the intrinsic value of the rights afforded by the put option contract are worth $15 per share to the owner of the put option contract. The owner of the put option has the contracted right to sell the underlying security to the seller of the put option for $50, $15 more than the current market price of $35.

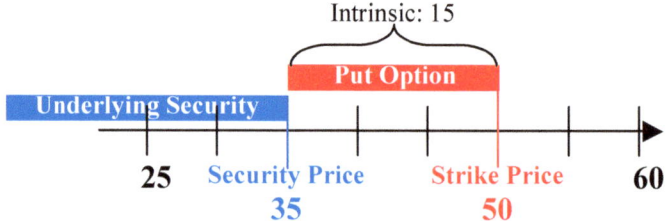

For example: If a call option contract was sold at a strike price of $50, and 100 shares of the underlying security are trading at $54, the rights afforded the buyer of the call option contract have an intrinsic value of $4 per share. The buyer of the call option contract can buy 100 shares of the underlying security from the seller of the call option contract for $50 and immediately sell it in the market for the current price of $54.

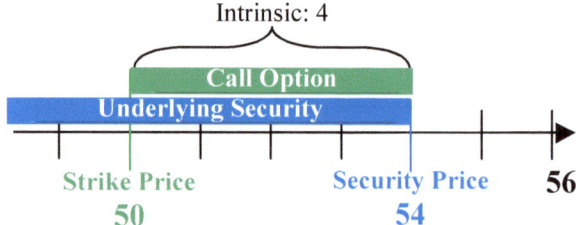

Option contract premiums have both intrinsic and time value components.

(vi) **Time Value** is indefinable value created through the forces of supply and demand, where more demand for an option contract at a particular strike price will increase its time value and more supply of an option contract at a particular strike price will decrease its time value. Buyer overpayment for option contracts is the time value (speculative value) portion of the premium.

For example: Referring to the following diagram, the total premium amount that the seller of the $50 strike price call option contract receives from the buyer is $4.50. $4.00 is the intrinsic value and $0.50 is the time value of the contract. The buyer of the call option contract has overpaid by $0.50, because the true value of a call option is measured as the distance between the option strike price and the security price when the security price is greater than the strike price. When the security price is less than the strike price the premium amount is only time value.

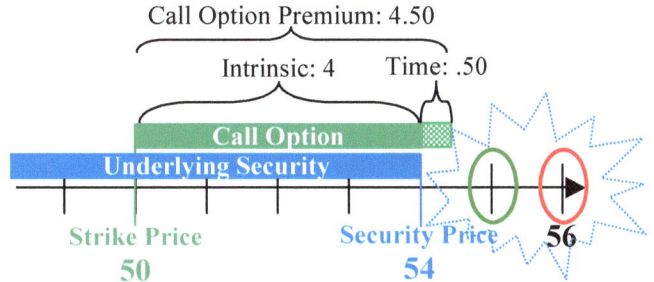

In this strategy, a short call spread will be created by selling a call option with a strike price at 55 (the green circle) and buying a hedging call option with a strike price of 56 (the red circle).

(vii) **Multiplier** for option contracts is 100--the amount that the quoted price of an option must be multiplied by to calculate the transaction dollar amount of the option contract, because the contract controls 100 shares of the underlying security.

For example: If the quoted price of an option contract is $12.15, the transaction amount will be $12.15 x 100 = $1215.00. One must also remember that each option contract controls or obligates 100 shares of the underlying security. If the underlying security is priced at $116.40, 100 shares at a transaction amount of $11640.00 (calculated as $116.40 x 100) will have to be purchased to cover an option contract's obligation when it is sold.

Another option contract of the same type (such as a call for a call or a put for a put) can be used as the hedging option in place of the 100 underlying security shares, because each purchased option contract provides the buyer with control over 100 shares at a fraction of the cost to owning the 100 shares. Control over 100 shares comes in two forms: first as the opportunity to exercise the rights of the option contract to sell or purchase 100 shares of the underlying security; and second, through price movements equal or fractionally equal to the price movements of the underlying security. The second definition of control found in option contracts is what makes them an outstanding source of *leverage*.

For example: The prior example lists the transaction price for 100 shares of an underlying security at $11640.00. The option contract price is only $1215.00. The option produces price movements equal to or fractionally equal to the price movements of the underlying security. Assuming that the price movements of this option contract are 2 to 1 or ½ that of the underlying security, a $2 price move in the underlying security creates a profit of $200 from 100 shares, for a return of 1.7% (calculated as $200 profit divided by $11640.00). The option contract profit is ½ that of the underlying security, so instead of a $200 profit, the option contraction realizes a $100 profit. The option contract return is 8.2% (calculated as $100 profit divided by $1215.00).

The option contract at its 2 to 1 or ½ price movement handicap returned a greater profit percentage than the 100 shares of the underlying security. This is an example of the leveraging power that option contracts provide.

(viii)   **Option Profits** are realized when the underlying security trades either up, down or flat, depending on one's ownership interest or position obligation in an option contract. Since option contracts can be purchased or sold, sellers of call options and buyers of put options realize profits when the underlying security falls in value. Buyers of call options and sellers of put options realize profits when the underlying security rises in value.

For example: When a put option is sold the put option looses value for the seller of the option when the underlying security falls in value, though the contract itself rises in value. Sellers of options seek the opposite result to buyers of options. If the underlying security were to rise in value, the seller of the put option will gain value while the buyer of the call option loses value.

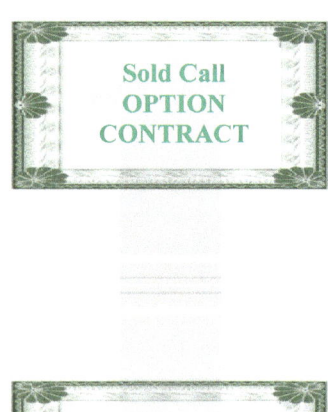

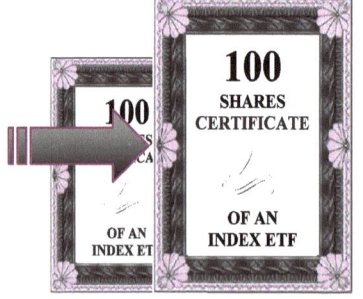

The components of a short spread and the value movements of the underlying security can be observed in the same way. As the value of the Index ETF falls, the short put spread looses value for the seller. The short call spread gains value for the seller. The following visualization represents this.

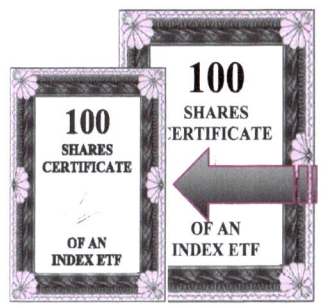

Though the contract value of the short put option is rising, sellers of options and short spreads seek the opposite result, therefore the seller's value is falling. Sellers of short spreads profit when the price difference between the sold option and purchased option shrinks or narrows, causing the spread to fall in value.

For example: If the initial price of the sold put option is $8.75 and the initial price of the purchased put option is $8.00, the spread value is $0.75 (calculated as the purchased option price from the sold option price, or $8.75 minus $8.00). Sellers of short spreads profit when the spread value falls or narrows so it can be purchased back at a lower price.

As the price of the Index ETF falls toward the strike prices of the short spread's component puts, the sold put option can gain $0.80 to $9.55 in value and the purchased put option can gain $0.55 to $8.55 in value. The spread value is now $1.00. It has increased when compared to its initial value of $0.75. The result for the spread seller is a $0.25 loss (calculated as $1.00 from $0.75).

Sellers of call and put options with no intrinsic value (only time value) in the option premium realize profits when the underlying security trades flat or away from the short spread. This strategy seeks to exploit that advantage for derivative income profit.

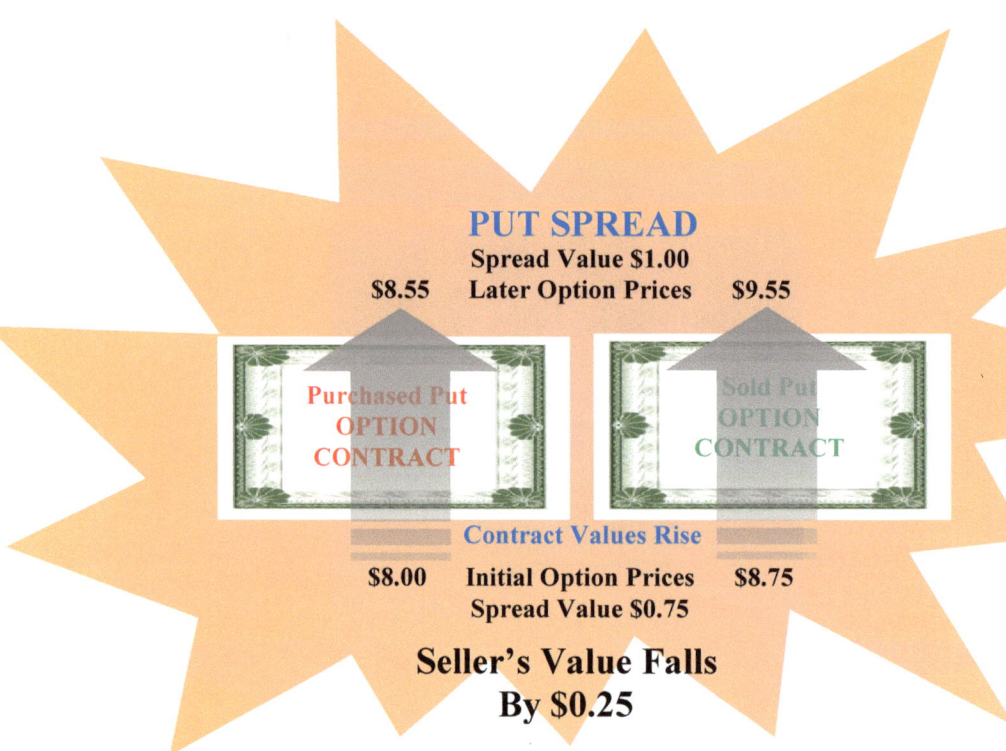

How Does The Spread Hedge Work?

As stated before, option contracts can hedge other option contracts. The contractual commitments created by options can be covered in ways other than owning 100 shares of the underlying security (obligated security) or by holding cash equal to the price of 100 shares of the underlying security when hedging the short put.

This strategy uses a hedging option that is purchased to hedge the dominant (higher priced) sold option. The dominant sold option also provides a shallow hedge for the encompassing short spread (the combined sold option and the purchased option). The risk obligation for a sold call option is infinite without a hedging option, because in theory the price of the underlying security can rise to infinity. The obligation for a sold put option is finite. Its value of the underlying security can only fall as far as zero.

The description of a spread (the cent unit difference between the component option strike prices) defines the *approximate risk*. If the spread is a $1 spread, the approximate risk is $100 (calculated as $1 multiplied by the 100 multiplier). The *defined risk* or *exact risk* of a spread is calculated as the approximate risk less the spread value.

For example: If the component option contracts of a short $1 spread cost $2.15 (sold put) and $2.05 (purchased put), the proceeds from each of the sold spread option contracts are

...an investing newsletter of general, impersonal and indirect opinion

$0.10 (calculated as $2.15 minus $2.05). $10 (calculated as $0.10 multiplied by 100 (the multiplier)) is the spread value or premium received from the sale of the spread. The exact risk of the spread is now definable as $90, the approximate risk of $100 (calculated as $1 (the spread description) multiplied by 100 (the multiplier)) less the spread value of $10. It is the premium income of $0.10 from the dominant option contract (the sold option contract in short spreads) that hedges the spread by reducing the defined risk to $90 from $100.

Trading accounts utilizing this strategy must hold in reserve cash equal to the amount of a spread's defined risk. The spread hedge provides leverage by lowering the definable risk (in the prior example, to $90 from $100).

What Is The Covering Margin?

The *covering margin* is the amount of money that must be maintained in a trading account to cover the potential loss obligation of a short spread. The covering margin is equal to the defined risk amount (calculated as the spread description (the cent unit difference between the strike prices of the sold option and the hedging option) minus the short spread premium value).

When options are used to hedge options, owning 100 shares of the underlying security or holding cash in an amount sufficient to purchase 100 shares of the underlying security at the contracted strike price is no longer necessary. Spread obligations can now be settled with cash held in reserve in the amount of the covering margin. The covering margin cash requirement facilitates leverage in this strategy, because it is less than the approximate risk amount (the spread width) and is a fraction of the cash required to own 100 shares of the underlying security.

For example: The prior example concludes that $90 is the covering margin for a short $1 spread that produces $10 in spread premium. The maximum return for this spread is 10% (calculated as $10 (the spread premium) divided by $100 (the approximate risk (calculated as $1 (the spread width) multiplied by the 100 multiplier). Leverage is provided from the spread hedge and subsequent covering margin amount, because the leveraged return (the yield) is calculated as $10 (the spread premium (derivative income)) divided by $90 (covering margin) for a yield of 11.1%.

Yield is a calculated percentage higher than a return. It uses leverage to create the same amount of profit with fewer dollar inputs.

What Is A Hedge Point?

The *hedge point* is the point at which the potential loss obligation becomes the realized loss obligation. It is located to the left of the short put option strike price in a short put spread and to the right of the short call option strike price in a short call spread. Its location on the underlying security value spectrum, calculated for a short put spread as the short spread proceeds ($0.10 from the prior examples) subtracted from the short option strike price (not defined in the prior examples). The long call spread calculates it as the short spread proceeds added to the short option strike price (not defined in the prior examples (see strategy diagram, page 3, for visualization)).

Loss can occur if the market price of the underlying security moves beyond the hedge point. This strategy tolerates small losses beyond the hedge point up to an amount designated as the stop loss point (usually chosen as twice the target monthly return), at which time the spread is purchased back from the market at a small loss.

How Does This Strategy Become Profitable?

There is one way to profit from this strategy. At market close on the 3rd Friday of every month, termed *option expiration*, the price of the underlying security (an Index ETF) must settle within the range boundary created by the short options of the short spreads (put and call spreads (see strategy diagram, page 3)). The short call option must be to the right of the Index ETF market price and the short put option must be to the left of the Index ETF market price (see strategy diagram, page 3).

If the market price of the Index ETF falls beyond the boundaries established by these dominant sold options, full potential profit will not be realized and losses can occur.

The profits from this strategy can be increased through the process of *rolling the spread*. Since this strategy is positioned at both sides of the underlying security, there is a 2 out of 3 chance that rolling the spread can occur at least once during the option cycle ending the 3rd Friday of every month. Why is rolling the spread profitable? Over time, option contracts lose value and eventually expire worthless if the option contract buyer's rights are not exercised. To option sellers, this result is profitable!

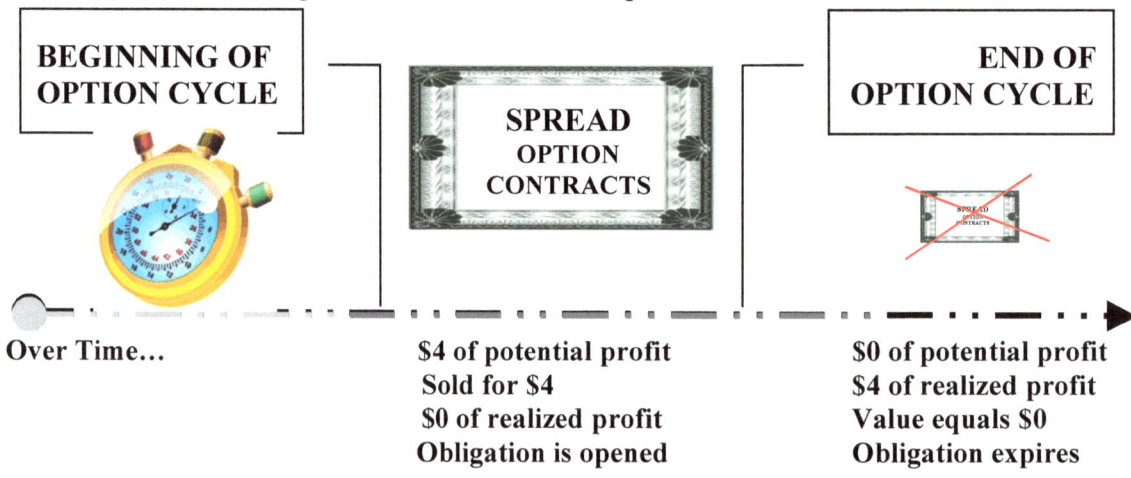

Over Time…	**$4 of potential profit**	**$0 of potential profit**
	Sold for $4	**$4 of realized profit**
	$0 of realized profit	**Value equals $0**
	Obligation is opened	**Obligation expires**

When the short put spread and short call spread at the ends of the profit zone fall in value, one or both spreads can be purchased in the market at less than it (the spread) or they (the spreads) were sold in order to cancel the initial sold option contract('s') obligation(s) — realizing profit for the seller of the option contract(s), as illustrated below.

A put option contract will lose value if the underlying security price moves away from the put option strike price. Whenever the price of the Index ETF moves up in value, the put option contracts to its left will lose value, allowing the combined option contracts of the put spread to be purchased for less than they were sold — again, making profit for the seller of the short put spread, as illustrated below.

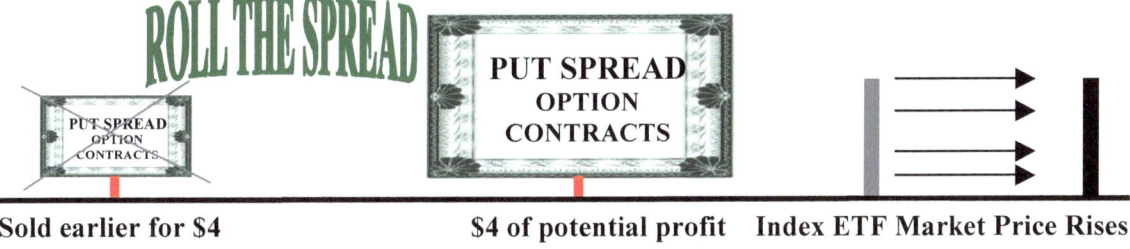

Sold earlier for $4	$4 of potential profit	Index ETF Market Price Rises
Purchased now for $1	$0 of realized profit	
$3 of realized profit	Sold now for $4	
Obligation is closed	Obligation is opened	

At the appropriate time, the initial short spread is purchased back for less than it was sold, and another short spread having greater value closer to the market price of the Index ETF is sold.

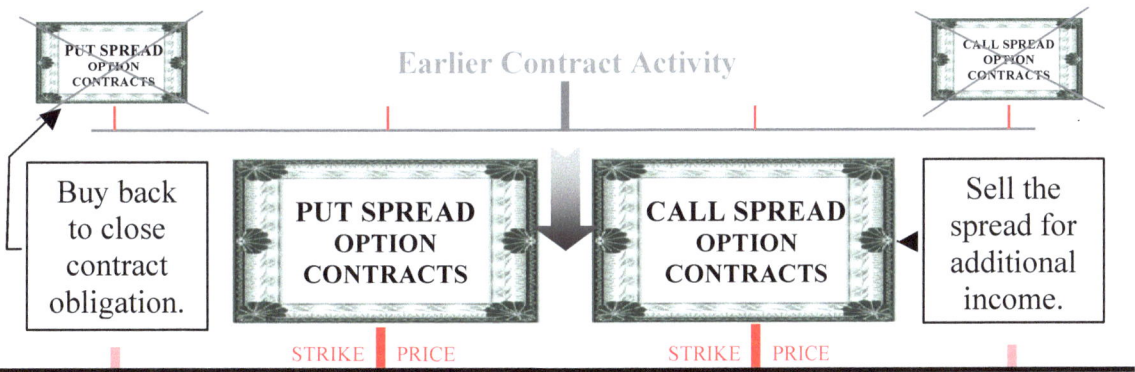

Later Contract Activity

What Is The Reward?

The reward is derivative income that can be expected in 95 out of 100 option cycles. This is a statistically significant number as determined by its location 2 standard deviations from the current market price of the Index ETF when the strategy is initiated. 2 standard deviations give a 95% probability that the market price of the Index ETF will close within the profit zone on option expiration between the boundaries established by the short option strike prices.

The target option cycle (the monthly) return is 4%, which can be increased by the number of rolling the spread opportunities (or decreased by Index ETF market price movements greater than 2 standard deviations in an option cycle).

Because option prices are influenced by market volatility, option cycles marked by low volatility may not produce derivative income opportunities at option strike prices located 2 standard deviations from the current underlying security market price. A careful study of implied price movements will inform whether this strategy should proceed at option strike prices closer to the underlying security market price (read the Hedge Strategies report, Technical Analysis Techniques For Timing The Market).

What Are The Risks?

The short spread hedge does not provide a significant reduction of risk. In fact, its purpose is two-fold and does not fall under the typical definition of a hedge. First, it facilitates the benefit of leverage in the spread. Without it, the high monthly returns of this strategy would not be possible. Second, it protects the spread seller from adverse obligations approaching an infinite dollar amount. In theory, the Index ETF market price could climb forever, making the loss from the sold call option unlimited.

Gapping in the Index ETF market price can occur, a result from the Index ETF price moving up or down, so far, so fast, that a stop loss order closes and exits the losing spread position at a loss greater than planned. As a Guidepost, the stop loss is set at a percentage equal to two months' average return for this strategy. If the Index ETF market price moves beyond either the put spread or call spread hedge points, the stop loss will be activated to protect the covering margin amount of the spread position.

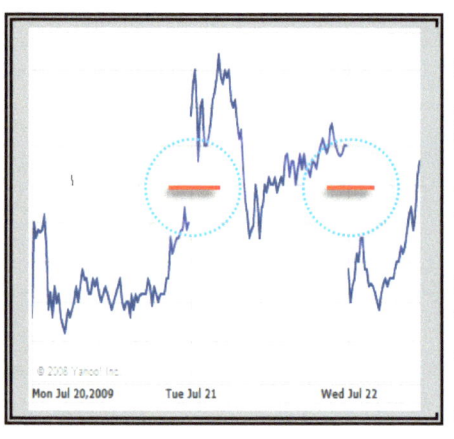

© 2008 Yahoo! Inc.
Mon Jul 20,2009   Tue Jul 21   Wed Jul 22

As the Index ETF market price moves away from one spread, in which this strategy produces harvestable profit, its movement toward the other spread erodes profit. The spread approached by the moving Index ETF market price loses profit faster than the spread at the other end gains profit. Markets that trade flat with little directional movement are the preferred condition for this strategy. In other words, when the market is experiencing particularly high volatility as measured by any of the specific market fear indices, large price movements are likely to be the norm during that option cycle. This strategy should not be initiated during that cycle, because the chance of the Index ETF market price moving beyond the boundaries established by the sold options is increased due to high market volatility (high price movements). The appropriate action is to move monies into the Hedged Income Index ETF conservative strategy (this strategy report also available for purchase) until market volatility subsides.

Outline Of A Monthly Moderate Hedging Strategy

Annual returns in both bear and bull markets can range from 38% to 73%, the latter including anticipated rolling the spread opportunities. This is a strategy that utilizes a double entry trade and as many rolling the spread trades as prudent per option cycle. The cost of these trades is not factored into return percentages, but could be as high as $1.50 for each action. Opening each short spread (put-side and call-side), which includes selling an option and purchasing a hedging option, is considered two actions. With double entry trades the cost of trades for each short condor can be $6. Rolling the spread on one wing of this strategy involves closing the initial spread and opening another spread closer to the market price of the Index ETF, an additional $6 cost of trades.

This strategy must be applied in a margin available account. If one were to initiate this strategy with a $1,000 covering margin position (incorrectly termed the investment amount), prior to any rolling the spread opportunities, the cost of trades could potentially be 17% of the annual return, or limit the annual return to 31.5% from 38%. Naturally, as one's available covering margin position increases, the cost of trades decreases significantly. A $10,000 covering margin position prior to any rolling the spread opportunities suffers a 1.7% cost of trades, which decreases the potential annual return to 37.35% from 38%, and for a $100,000 covering margin position to just 37.93% from 38%.

Entry Trade
Step 1: Sell an Index ETF Call Spread and an Index ETF Put Spread that complies with the Boundary Guidepost for a monthly income yield of approximately 4%.
Step 2: Establish the stop losses.

Rolling the Spread (when profitable)
Step 3: Close the profitable Spread(s) by purchasing it(them) for a profit.
Step 4: Sell closer to the Index ETF market price Spread(s) complying with the Boundary Guidepost for an income yield of approximately 4%.
Step 5: Reset the stop loss(es).
Step 6: Repeat Step 3 when profitable and in compliance with the Boundary Guidepost.

Boundary Guidepost
The amount that the market price of an Index ETF is likely to move is predicted using the variables of (i) market specific volatility, (ii) data from specific Index ETF options, (iii) 2

...an investing newsletter of general, impersonal and indirect opinion

standard deviations calculations, and (iv) bullish or bearish market sentiment. These variables are part of the analysis that justifies the width of the profit range (or the strike prices at which the short option boundaries are to be established).

The first and most important calculation is the 2 standard deviations determination. Its result provides a boundary range that must be justified by additional market analysis. What is a 2 standard deviations boundary? It is a measure of probability that states that the market price of a derivative or security will close within the resulting profit zone (range) 95.449 times out of 100.

The following formulas will return the 2 standard deviations boundary range values 30 days from option expiration for an Index ETF if one has the Index ETF current market price and implied volatility value (available at option brokerages). The implied volatility value for an Index ETF is approximated by the implied volatility value of the call option with strike price closest to the Index ETF market price in the option cycle with the nearest expiration date. The lower boundary is determined as:

$$\textbf{market price} - (\ (\ (\textbf{market price} \times (\textbf{implied volatility} \times 0.01)\ )\ ) \div 1.833)$$

The upper boundary is determined as:

$$\textbf{market price} + (\ (\ (\textbf{market price} \times (\textbf{implied volatility} \times 0.01)\ )\ ) \div 1.833)$$

The following formulas will return the 2 standard deviations boundary range values 7 days from option expiration for an Index ETF if one has the Index ETF current market price and implied volatility data (available at option brokerages). The lower boundary is determined as:

$$\textbf{market price} - (\ (\ (\textbf{market price} \times (\textbf{implied volatility} \times 0.01)\ )\ ) \div 2.683)$$

The upper boundary is determined as:

$$\textbf{market price} + (\ (\ (\textbf{market price} \times (\textbf{implied volatility} \times 0.01)\ )\ ) \div 2.683)$$

Interior range values between 30 and 7 days can now be extrapolated as a linear approximation.

Individual option contracts (especially those with high levels of trading volume) provide useful information about market sentiment. The specifics of this information are separated into variables identified by Greek symbols. Of particular interest is an option's delta (Δ). The delta suggests the degree to which the option price will change for every dollar change in the price of the underlying security. It also provides a measure of probability for the price of the underlying security meeting the strike price of the short option at the end of the option cycle.

For example: If the delta of a put option at a strike price is 70. The delta suggests a 70% probability that on expiration of the put option the price of the underlying security will close at or below the strike price of this put option. If the delta of a call option at a strike price is 5. The delta suggests a 5% probability that on expiration of the call option the price of the underlying security will close at or above the strike price of this call option.

The Chicago Board Options Exchange (CBOE) has created measures of market specific volatility for numerous indices like the DJIA and the S&P 500. Charting and technical analysis of these measures of market specific volatility provide valuable insight into the anticipated amplitude of near-term index movements. The level of volatility translates into an expected percentage value movement for the market within the following 30 days. As a check for boundary range (width) accuracy, one now may ask if this expected index value movement falls within the calculated 2 standard deviations boundary of the Index ETF. If it does not, move monies into the Hedged Income Index ETF conservative strategy (this strategy report also available for purchase) until market volatility subsides.

Introduced in 1993 on the S&P 100 and then converted to the S&P 500 in 2003, the derivative, symbol VIX, is the measure of volatility for the S&P 500 index. The VIX measures the implied volatility of prices for S&P 500 index options. Implied volatility is itself a short term measure of demand-driven price inflation for options, signaling the intent to use index options to hedge portfolios against loss in long investments or short positions. Though typically read as a measure for possible market declines, the VIX can also signal the movement of market values upward.

An additional calculation is applied to the VIX to determine the 30-day anticipated value movement percentage for the S&P 500 index. The resulting percentage movement can be either up, down or a range composed of both up and down movements. The calculation produces a possible percentage value movement, within the following 30 days, that has a 68% probability of occurring. The following chart of calculations shows the resulting possible percentage value movements for the S&P 500 index (the right column) when the VIX returns the following values (the left column). Interior range values can be extrapolated as a linear approximation.

The following graph plots the S&P 500 from October 24th to November 24th, 2008. As a test, the October 24, 2008 VIX high outlier of 89.53 calculation is observed for predictive accuracy. The 89.53 VIX value suggests that there is a 68% chance that there will be a price movement of 25.85% in the S&P 500 index either up, down or in combination within the following 30 days.

VIX Values		Possible 30-day 68% probable percentage value movements for the S&P 500 Index
15	-	4.33%
Average 19.04	-	5.50% 1990 - October 2008
20	-	5.77%
40	-	11.55%
60	-	17.32%
80	-	23.09%
High 89.53	-	25.85% October 24, 2008

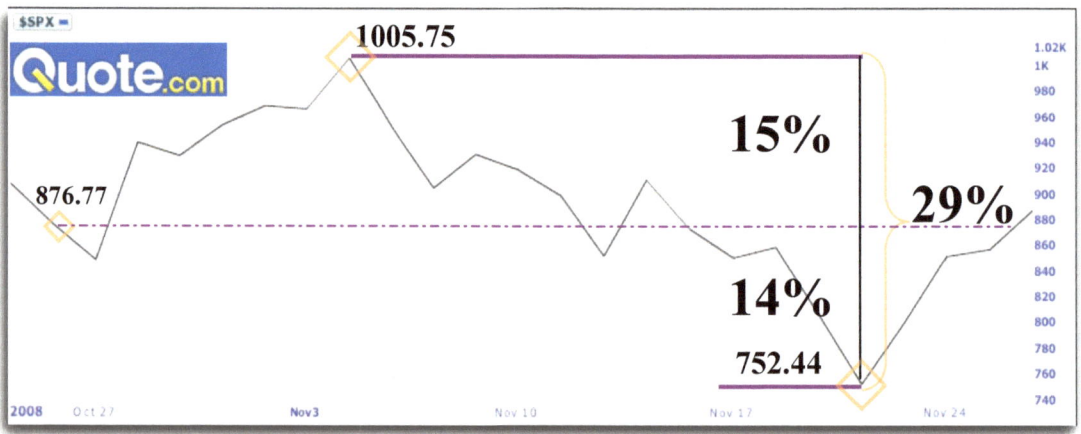

As predicted, the S&P 500 index moved dramatically by high percentages in both directions. Combined, the maximum resulting value movement in the 30-day period between October 24 and November 24 was 29%. The VIX based value movement calculation was off by only 12% from the actual.

The 2 standard deviations calculation, option deltas, and VIX calculations create a corroborative estimation for the price movements of an underlying security. Market sentiment is a useful variable for confirming the adequacy of the profit zone boundary range. During bullish periods prices tend to rise at a slow to moderate pace—a desired movement for this applied moderate strategy. However, during bearish periods prices can fall suddenly. This phenomenon is confirmed by the S&P 500 index chart below. What took many years to gain was lost in a fraction of the time. Sudden price movements are not desired for this strategy.

Stop Loss Percentage Guidepost

If the market price of the Index ETF moves beyond the hedge point, covering margin losses will occur. The hedge for this strategy is shallow and provides limited protection. Two triggering events can be established that will activate the stop loss to close the threatened spread. The first is the Index ETF market price reaching the strike price of the short option. The second is the average Net Profit return percentage falling below two option cycles' cumulative returns. If option cycle target derivative income is 4%, the trigger for the stop loss is set at -8%. Statistically, the stop loss should be triggered 5 out of 100 option cycles or 5 months in eight years and four months.

Derivative Income Uses Guidepost

This applied moderate strategy produces immediate cash flows from the short spreads' premium values. How should these cash flows be used? These cash flows will be maintained as part of the covering margin amount, facilitating leveraged income profits.

Test Results For July 2009 - Example 1

The first example is an application of this strategy that does not roll the spread. The underlying security is the S&P 500 Index ETF, which holds a moderate level of volatility when compared to other indices. The current market conditions hold volatility above the historic average and a bearish sentiment.

The market price of the Index ETF at time of entry is $92.70. The Boundary Guidepost places the strategy's short options at strike prices of 82 and 99 and the hedging options one strike beyond, making $1 spreads. The put spread is sold for a $4 premium and the call spread is sold for a $5 premium. The covering margin is $96 for the short put spread and $95 for the short call spread.

The potential derivative profit return for this month's option cycle period is 4.5% (see following chart) on the combined short spreads. The spreads are leveraged, so the yield is 4.7% (calculated as $((4 + 5) \div 2) \div 95.5)$), because the covering margin risked in this trade is the average of both put spread and call spread covering margins, (95.5, calculated as ((96 + 95) ÷ 2)), not 100.

As the market price of the Index ETF falls, moving away from the short call spread, the call spread becomes profitable. On July 8, the market price of the Index ETF turns and begins to move upward, allowing the short put spread to become profitable. There is little chance that option contracts will have time (speculative) value in the final five days of their lives. Time value is a function of trading activity. There will be no buyers interested in trading option contracts with such a short lifespan. Though the price of the underlying security changes direction on July 8, it does not stimulate a rise in time value for this short call spread.

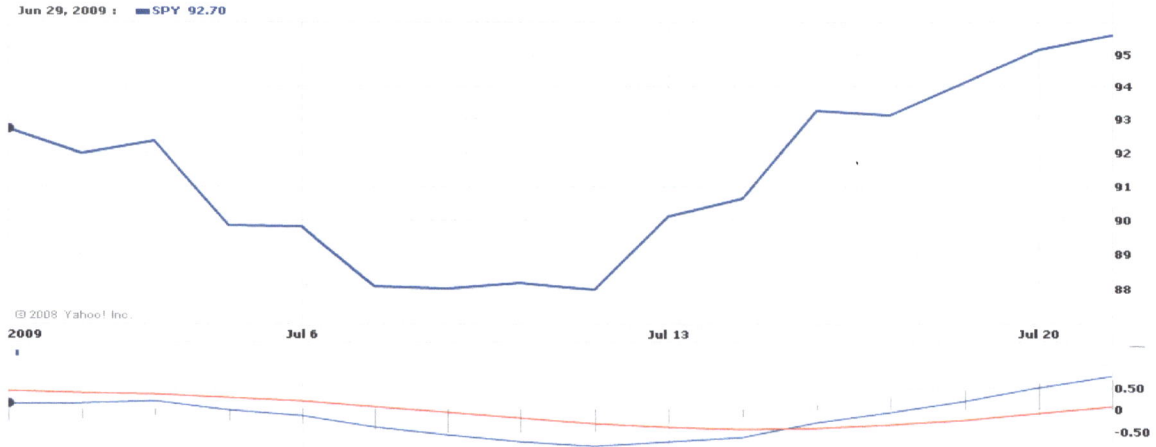

Reproduced with permission of Yahoo! Inc. ©2010 Yahoo! Inc. YAHOO! and the YAHOO! logo are registered trademarks of Yahoo! Inc.

SPY			Put Spread			Call Spread			Derivative Profit 4.5%
Days To Expiration	Date	ETF Price	81	Derivative Income	82	99	Derivative Income	100	Net Profit
18	29-Jun	92.70	13	--	17	11	--	6	0.0%
17	30-Jun	91.95	13	0	17	8	3	6	1.5%
16	1-Jul	92.33	14	3	15	9	2	6	2.5%
15	2-Jul	89.81	18	-1	23	5	2	2	0.5%
11	6-Jul	89.80	14	1	17	3	5	3	3.0%
10	7-Jul	88.06	20	-2	26	2	4	1	1.0%
9	8-Jul	88.00	19	-2	25	2	4	1	1.0%
8	9-Jul	88.17	11	-1	16	1	5	1	2.0%
7	10-Jul	87.96	8	0	12	2	4	1	2.0%
4	13-Jul	90.10	3	3	4	1	5	1	4.0%
3	14-Jul	90.61	2	4	2	1	5	1	4.5%
2	15-Jul	93.26	1	4	1	2	5	2	4.5%
1	16-Jul	93.11	1	4	1	1	5	1	4.5%
EXPIRED	17-Jul	94.13	1	4	1	1	5	1	4.5%

Spread specific profit was experienced in this trade on July 6 for the short call spread (outlined in green). Though it was not done in this example, as early as four days into the trade the call spread could have been rolled to harvest profit, and reestablished for additional derivative income, provided that these actions comply with the Boundary Guidepost.

Test Results For August 2009 - Example 2
The second example uses the same S&P 500 Index ETF as its underlying security and applies the strategy shortly after the close of the prior option cycle. The current market conditions hold volatility slightly above its historic average. The market sentiment is bullish.

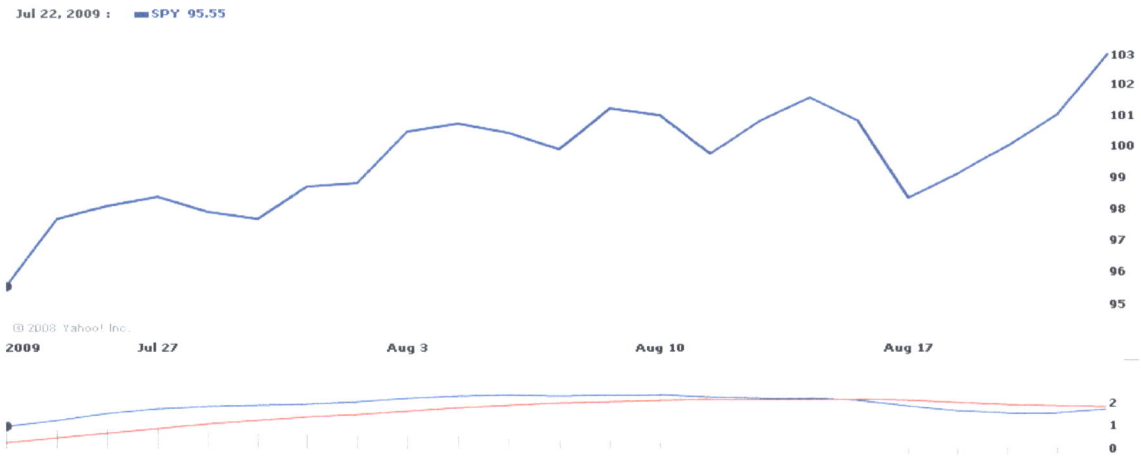

Reproduced with permission of Yahoo! Inc. ©2010 Yahoo! Inc. YAHOO! and the YAHOO! logo are registered trademarks of Yahoo! Inc.

Remember that short spread value loss is this strategy's objective. In order to demonstrate the opportunities for profit harvesting in the face of position value loss, target derivative income is set at 4% for both the short put spread and short call spread. This example will allow for *rolling the spread* activities to increase derivative income after a period of passive trading. The stop loss is set at –8%, averaged from the anticipated option cycle (monthly) derivative income from the short put and short call option spreads, twice the target net profit return.

The bullish sentiment lifts the Index ETF market price quickly toward the short call spread, causing strategy losses to the call spread at twice the amount of the gains to the short put spread. Note the spreadsheet cells filled with yellow in the Derivative Income column. Opportunities for harvesting put spread profits by rolling the spread occurred 3 times (outlined with green) prior to August 4. Note how positioning short spreads at either end of the market slowed the Net losses (column to the far right). The call spread loss on August 4 reached -$14, but the put spread gain of $3 limited the average net profit decline to just -5.5%, still below the Stop Loss triggering percentage of -8%.

Rolling the spread occurred at the short put spread on August 4. $3 of Derivative Income was harvested and added to the covering margin to increase leverage for the new 91 / 92 short put spread, recharged with $4 of potential derivative income profit. Why was there a failure to harvest the total 4 units of the short put spread's potential profit instead of the $3 highlighted with green on August 4? The obligation of an option contract cannot be closed for zero dollars except by contract expiration at the end of the option cycle. One dollar is the minimum amount needed to close an option contract.

Threatening price movements toward the short call spread eased on August 5, beginning a period of range-bound (flat) trading. The short put spread was harvested for income twice more. August 17 represents a price decline through support. This downside price movement raised the value of the put spread, reflected in the -$13 loss to Derivative Income (outlined with red). Spread sellers realize profits when the options of spreads fall in value.

The strategy return was 8.5% (more than twice the target). The yield was 8.85%.

SPY			Put Spread			Call Spread			Derivative Profit 4%
Days To Expiration	Date	ETF Price	83	Derivative Income	84	105	Derivative Income	106	Net Profit
30	22-Jul	95.55	16	--	20	13	--	9	0.0%
29	23-Jul	97.66	12	2	14	26	-3	19	-0.5%
28	24-Jul	98.06	10	4	10	29	-4	21	0.0%
25	27-Jul	98.35	8	2	10	31	-8	19	-3.0%
24	28-Jul	97.89	11	1	14	26	-4	18	-1.5%
23	29-Jul	97.79	13	2	15	25	-4	17	-1.0%
22	30-Jul	98.67	10	4	10	31	-5	22	-0.5%
21	31-Jul	98.81	6	2	8	32	-4	24	-1.0%
18	3-Aug	100.44	6	4	6	52	-12	36	-4.0%
17	4-Aug	100.70	4	3	5	51	-14	33	-5.5%
17	4-Aug	100.70	91	4%	92	--	--	--	--
16	5-Aug	100.41	13	0	17	38	-9	25	-3.0%
15	6-Aug	99.89	17	-1	22	32	-8	20	-3.0%
14	7-Aug	101.20	12	2	14	38	-7	27	-1.0%
11	10-Aug	100.99	9	3	10	30	-7	19	-0.5%
11	10-Aug	100.99	92	4%	93	--	--	--	--
10	11-Aug	99.73	14	0	18	12	0	8	3.0%
9	12-Aug	100.80	10	2	12	15	0	11	4.0%
8	13-Aug	101.57	6	2	8	21	-8	9	0.0%
7	14-Aug	100.79	5	3	6	9	0	5	4.5%
7	14-Aug	100.79	95	4%	96	--	--	--	--
4	17-Aug	98.31	31	-13	48	3	2	1	1.0%
3	18-Aug	99.09	12	-2	18	3	3	2	5.0%
2	19-Aug	99.96	6	2	8	2	3	1	7.0%
1	20-Aug	100.99	2	4	2	1	4	1	8.5%
EXPIRED	21-Aug	102.97	1	4	1	1	4	1	8.5%

Why It's Done This Way

Although one can apply the spreads of this Short Condor strategy in a manner that yields even higher monthly gains, chances of loss and chances of returns are inversely related, so higher returns will also create greater frequencies of loss. This strategy is designed to increase the probabilities of reward to risk, decrease market price movement risk and provide consistent monthly derivative income.

Amplitude

A physicist knows that amplitude is the maximum deviation of an alternating current from its average value. A derivatives trader understands that risk to this Short Condor strategy is defined purely by the amplitude of market price movements, not the direction of market price movements.

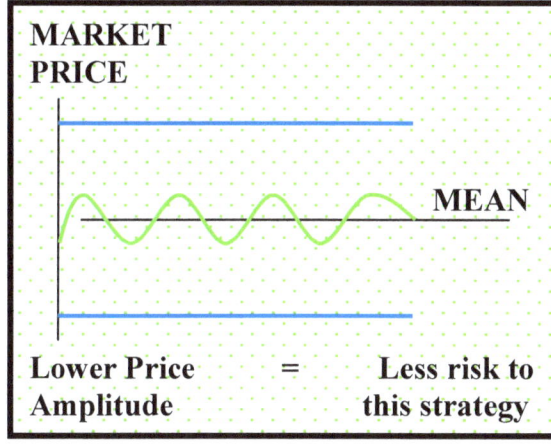
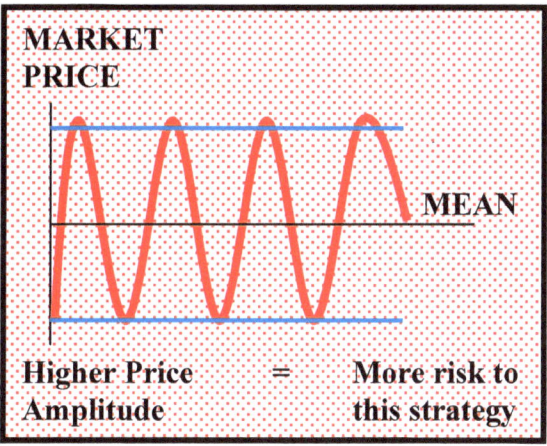

The indicators that predict amplitudinal market price movements are the volatility indicators as described in the Guidepost section titled Boundary Guidepost (page 17).

On Choosing The Best Strategy For A Portfolio

Risk is not knowing the outcome of an investment or position. In the spectrum of investment or position strategies some are defined as more risky than others. Buy and hold strategies are far more risky than derivative hedging strategies. What makes a strategy risky? An investment or position strategy is incomplete if it has only a plan for entering the market. The complete investment or position strategy also details methods for daily monitoring and for exiting the market. Without these plans, any investment or position strategy is risky. With them the riskiest strategies can be made less risky.

How Will A Portfolio Utilizing This Strategy Look In The Future?

This strategy derives its strength in its consistency of return from a ratio of statistically defined successes to losses. The chart below provides a timeline for the number of months required to attain a one million dollar goal (taxes not considered if this is applied

…an investing newsletter of general, impersonal and indirect opinion

in a non-tax advantaged investment account) from the starting dollar amounts (without further contributions) at a modest monthly return of 4% compounded monthly.

Starting Amount	Months to 1 Million (5 Losses to 100)	Years
3,000	174	14.5
5,000	157	13.1
10,000	137	11.4
25,000	110	9.2
50,000	89	7.4
100,000	69	5.8

Doubles
21 Months

The starting amount doubles every 21 months (1 year and 9 months). This strategy does not suffer backtracking as a consequence of systematic (market price movement) risk. In other words, the ratio of expected losing months to winning months is not influenced by the direction of the market as a whole. When directionally traded investments like mutual funds are suffering in a falling market, this moderate strategy does not share their fate.

Questions regarding this material may be forwarded to help2hsc@HedgeStrategies.info.

<u>Additional Hedge Strategies Investing Reports</u>

 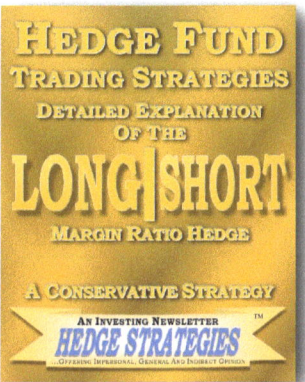 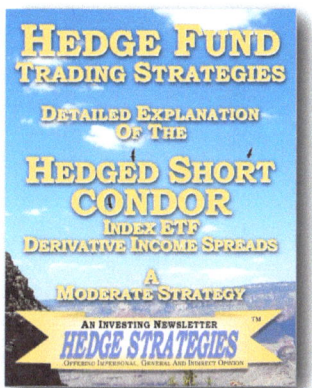

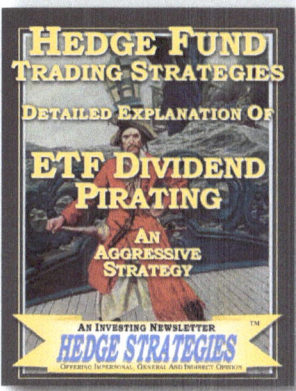 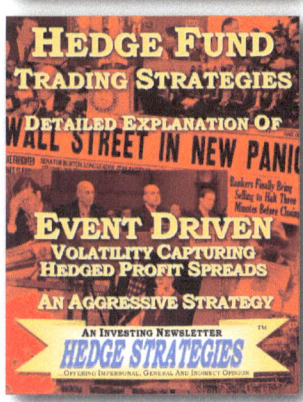 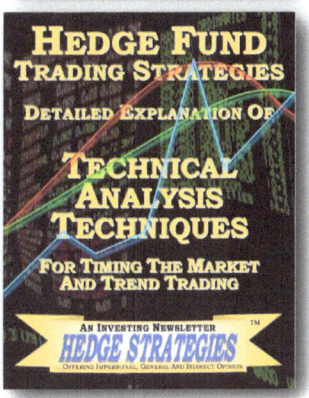

RISK DISCLOSURE STATEMENT

It should not be assumed that concepts, models or strategies discussed, presently or in the future, will always be profitable or will equal the performance of the strategy as explained in this report.

Transactions in options carry a high degree of risk. If the option is "covered" by the seller holding a corresponding position in the underlying security or a future contract or another option, the risk may be reduced. If the option is not covered, the risk of loss can be unlimited.

Most open-outcry and electronic trading facilities are supported by computer-based component systems for the order routing, execution, matching, registration or clearing of trades. As with all facilities and systems, they are vulnerable to temporary disruption or failure. Your ability to recover certain losses may be subject to limits on liability imposed by the system provider, the market, the clearing house and/or member firms. Such limits may vary. You can ask the firm with which you deal for details in this respect.

Trading on an electronic trading system may differ not only from trading in an open-outcry market, but also from trading on other electronic trading systems. If you undertake transactions on an electronic trading system, you will be exposed to risks associated with the system including the failure of hardware and software. The result of any system failure may be that your order is either not executed according to your instructions or is not executed at all.

www.ingramcontent.com/pod-product-compliance
Lightning Source LLC
Chambersburg PA
CBHW050425180526
45159CB00005B/2414